PRODUCTIVITY UNLEASHED

TIME MANAGEMENT STRATEGIES FOR ENTREPRENEURS

DR. MINAKSHI BANSAL

DEDICATION

To all the aspiring and established entrepreneurs who dare to dream big, work tirelessly, and never give up. May this book empower you to harness the power of time and achieve your wildest aspirations.

Contents

Contents

Contents

Prayer

"Om Bhadram Karnebhih Shrinuyama Devah

Bhadram Pashyemakshabhiryajatrah

Sthirairangais Tushtuvamsastanubhih

Vyashema Devahitam Yadayuh

Svasti Na Indro Vriddhashravah

Svasti Nah Pusha Vishwavedah

Svasti Nastarkshyo Arishtanemih

Svasti No Brihaspatir Dadhatu

Om Shantih Shantih Shantih"

This mantra is a prayer for universal well-being, invoking the blessings of various deities for protection, health, and happiness. It emphasizes the importance of experiencing the auspicious through all senses and living a life aligned with divine purpose. The repetition of "Shantih" at the end signifies a deep desire for peace in the individual, the environment, and the universe at large. This mantra is often recited as a prayer for peace, prosperity, and the physical and spiritual well-being of all beings.

ɣɣɣ

About The Author

This book represents the culmination of extensive research and meticulous analysis, incorporating a diverse range of sources, including numerous books, scholarly studies, and personal experiences. Additionally, I have scoured various websites to gather relevant information and data essential for the compilation of this work. I have taken every precaution to ensure the accuracy of the information presented and have diligently cited all sources to acknowledge their contributions.

From her earliest days, Minakshi was distinguished by an insatiable appetite for reading. Her literary universe was inhabited by characters and narratives that spanned ethical tales, motivational and inspirational stories, and the mythic parables imbued with life lessons. This voracious reading habit was not merely for personal edification but was driven by a desire to distill and disseminate the essence of these narratives to foster the development of students and peers alike. She was particularly captivated by the lives and teachings of historical figures and spiritual leaders such as Adi Shankaracharya, Swami Vivekananda, Dr. APJ Abdul Kalam, Mahamana Pandit Madan Mohan Malviya, Mahatma Gandhi, Sardar Vallabhai Patel, and Vinoba Bhave, among others. Their philosophies and life stories fueled her ambition to embody their ideals of resilience, selflessness, and relentless pursuit of knowledge.

Dr. Minakshi's academic and practical engagement with psychology has been equally noteworthy. As a research scholar, her focus has been on exploring the intricate tapestry of the human psyche, aiming to unlock the potential for psychological well-being and societal harmony. Her scholarly work is complemented by her active involvement in social work, where she employs her academic insights to make tangible differences in the lives of the underprivileged. Her endeavours in social work are characterized by an innovative approach that combines traditional wisdom with contemporary psychological practices to address the multifaceted challenges faced by these communities.

Her artistic talents, another facet of her diverse capabilities, are not merely a personal passion but also serve as a medium through which she communicates and connects with others. Her art, rich in symbolism and emotional depth, reflects her philosophical inquiries and social concerns, offering viewers a glimpse into the breadth of her intellect and the depth of her compassion.

In addition to her contributions to the arts and social sciences, Dr. Minakshi has embraced the healing arts of Pranic Healing, mastering the techniques developed by Master Choa Kok Sui. This practice, which focuses on the manipulation of Prana or life energy to heal the body and aura, has been both a personal journey of discovery and a means through which she extends her healing touch to others. Her proficiency in Pranic Healing is complemented by her advocacy and teaching of various forms of meditation aimed at rejuvenation, personal betterment, and the cultivation of harmony within individuals and communities alike.

Dr. Minakshi's life is a narrative of relentless pursuit, not just of personal achievement but of the upliftment and empowerment of society at large. Her diverse interests and talents—spanning the arts, literature, psychology, and the healing practices—converge on a singular path of service. She embodies the spirit of the luminaries who inspired her, channelling their legacy through her actions and teachings. Through her books, art, and social initiatives, she continues to inspire a new generation to embark on their own journeys of self-discovery, resilience, and altruism.

Her commitment to social betterment, particularly her focus on uplifting underprivileged children, reflects a deep understanding of the transformative potential of education and personal development. By integrating her knowledge of psychology, her artistic sensibilities, and her healing practices, Dr. Bansal has developed a holistic approach to social work that addresses both the immediate needs and the long-term well-being of the communities she serves.

As an author, Dr. Minakshi's writings offer a blend of inspirational insights, practical wisdom, and reflective contemplations drawn from her extensive reading and life experiences. Her books serve as a guide for those seeking to navigate the complexities of life with grace, resilience, and purpose. Through her narratives, she extends an invitation to her readers to explore the depths of their own potential and to contribute meaningfully to the collective well-being of society.

In Dr. Minakshi Bansal, we find a remarkable synthesis of the artist, the scholar, the healer, and the social activist. Her life's work stands as a beacon of hope and a source of inspiration for individuals seeking to make a difference in the world. Her story is a compelling reminder of the power of individual action, rooted in compassion and driven by a profound commitment to the betterment of humanity. Dr. Minakshi's legacy is not just in the tangible outcomes of her efforts but in the enduring spirit of inquiry, empathy, and service that she embodies.

ᢕᢕᢕ

Preface

Embarking on the entrepreneurial journey is akin to setting sail on uncharted waters. It's a thrilling adventure filled with boundless possibilities, but it's also fraught with challenges and uncertainties. As I navigated these waters myself, I realized that one of the most critical factors in determining my success was my ability to manage my time effectively.

Time, as the saying goes, is money. But for entrepreneurs, it's much more than that. It's the lifeblood of our businesses, the fuel that powers our dreams. Every minute wasted is a missed opportunity, a potential setback. Yet, in the face of countless demands and distractions, mastering time management can feel like an elusive goal.

This realization sparked a deep dive into the world of productivity. I devoured books, attended seminars, and experimented with countless techniques and tools. Through trial and error, I discovered a set of strategies that not only transformed my own productivity but also helped countless other entrepreneurs achieve their goals.

This book is the culmination of that journey. It's a distillation of the most effective time management strategies that I've personally tested and refined over the years. It's not a one-size-fits-all solution, but rather a toolkit that you can adapt to your unique needs and circumstances.

The strategies presented here are not just about squeezing more tasks into your day. They're about working smarter, not harder. They're about prioritizing your most important tasks, eliminating distractions, and creating a sustainable workflow that fosters both personal and professional growth.

Whether you're a seasoned entrepreneur or just starting out, this book will provide you with the insights and tools you need to take control of your time, maximize your productivity, and achieve your entrepreneurial dreams.

I've structured the book into a series of chapters, each focusing on a specific aspect of time management. You'll learn how to set clear goals, prioritize tasks, manage distractions, delegate effectively, and leverage technology to streamline your workflow. You'll also discover the power of routines, breaks, and stress management in maintaining peak performance.

Throughout the book, I'll share personal anecdotes and case studies from my own entrepreneurial journey, as well as insights from other successful entrepreneurs. I believe that these real-world examples will help you to relate to the material and apply the strategies to your own life and business.

I'm confident that this book will be a valuable resource for you as you navigate the challenges and opportunities of entrepreneurship. It's my hope that the strategies and insights shared here will empower you to take control of your time, achieve your goals, and live a more fulfilling and productive life.

Remember, time is your most valuable asset. Don't let it slip away. Use it wisely, invest it strategically, and watch your entrepreneurial dreams become a reality.

Dr. Minakshi Bansal
Social Activist
Ahmedabad, Gujarat, Bharat

ppp

ONE

THE ENTREPRENEURIAL CLOCK: WHY TIME IS YOUR MOST VALUABLE ASSET.

In the realm of entrepreneurship, time is a currency unlike any other. It's the most valuable asset you possess, yet it's finite and irreplaceable. While money can be earned, lost, and earned again, time once spent is gone forever. As an entrepreneur, your ability to master the art of time management is not just a skill; it's a superpower that can catapult your business to new heights.

The entrepreneurial clock ticks differently than a traditional 9-to-5 job. It's not bound by set hours or weekends. It's a relentless rhythm that demands your attention and energy, often blurring the lines between work and personal life. However, it's precisely this freedom and flexibility that make time management so crucial for entrepreneurs.

The value of time for an entrepreneur is multifaceted. First and foremost, it's the fuel that powers your business. Every minute you invest in your venture is a minute closer to achieving your goals. Whether it's brainstorming new ideas, developing products, marketing your services, or building relationships with clients, every action you take requires time.

Time is also a scarce resource. There are only 24 hours in a day, and how you allocate those hours can make or break your entrepreneurial journey. Every decision you make about how to spend your time has a direct impact on your productivity, efficiency, and ultimately, your success.

The opportunity cost of time is another factor that entrepreneurs must grapple with. Every minute you spend on one task is a minute you can't spend on another. This means that every choice you make has trade-offs. For example, if you choose to spend an hour responding to emails, you're sacrificing an hour that could have been used to develop a new marketing strategy or meet with a potential investor.

Moreover, time is a perishable asset. It doesn't wait for anyone. The longer you delay taking action, the more opportunities you miss. In the fast-paced world of entrepreneurship, time is of the essence. Procrastination and indecision can be costly, as competitors may seize the opportunities you hesitate to pursue.

The entrepreneurial clock is also a reflection of your personal values and priorities. How you choose to spend your time reveals what truly matters to you. As an entrepreneur, you have the freedom to design a life that aligns with your passions and aspirations. By consciously managing your time, you can ensure that your business and personal life are in harmony.

Mastering time management is not an overnight process. It requires self-awareness, discipline, and a willingness to experiment with different strategies. However, the rewards are immeasurable. When you harness the power of time, you gain the ability to:

Increase Productivity: By focusing on high-value activities and eliminating time-wasters, you can accomplish more in less time.

Enhance Efficiency: By streamlining processes and automating repetitive tasks, you can optimize your workflow and achieve better results.

Reduce Stress: By prioritizing tasks and avoiding overload, you can create a more manageable workload and reduce stress levels.

Improve Decision-Making: By understanding the opportunity cost of time, you can make more informed decisions about how to allocate your resources.

Achieve Work-Life Balance: By setting boundaries and protecting your personal time, you can create a fulfilling life both inside and outside of your business.

The entrepreneurial clock is a constant reminder that time is your most valuable asset. It's a challenge and an opportunity. By embracing the entrepreneurial clock and mastering time management, you can unlock your full potential, achieve your goals, and create a business and life that you love.

In the following chapters, we will delve deeper into the strategies and techniques that can help you harness the power of time. We will explore how to set goals, prioritize tasks, manage distractions, and leverage technology to streamline your workflow. We will also discuss the importance of self-care, delegation, and continuous learning.

By the end of this book, you will have a comprehensive toolkit for time management that you can tailor to your specific needs and goals. You will be equipped with the knowledge and skills to take control of your time, maximize your productivity, and unleash your entrepreneurial spirit. Remember, the clock is ticking. It's time to take charge and make the most of every minute. Your entrepreneurial success depends on it.

ᗡᗡᗡ

Time is the entrepreneur's most precious currency. Invest it wisely, spend it strategically, and watch your business flourish. Remember, every minute counts in the pursuit of your dreams.

TWO

GOAL SETTING: YOUR COMPASS FOR PRODUCTIVITY.

In the dynamic landscape of entrepreneurship, where opportunities abound and challenges constantly arise, having a clear direction is paramount. Goals serve as the compass that guides entrepreneurs through the turbulent waters of business, ensuring that their efforts are focused, intentional, and ultimately, successful.

Imagine embarking on a journey without a destination in mind. You might wander aimlessly, wasting precious time and resources, unsure of whether you're making progress or simply spinning your wheels. This is the predicament many entrepreneurs find themselves in when they neglect the power of goal setting. Without clear objectives, it's easy to become sidetracked by distractions, lose sight of the bigger picture, and succumb to the overwhelm of daily tasks.

Goals act as beacons, illuminating the path towards your desired outcomes. They provide a sense of purpose, motivation, and direction. When you know what you're working towards, every action you take becomes more meaningful and impactful. Goals also serve as benchmarks, allowing you to measure your progress and celebrate your achievements along the way.

Effective goal setting is not merely about writing down a wish list. It's a strategic process that requires careful thought, planning, and execution. The first step is to identify your long-term vision. What do you ultimately want to achieve with your business? Where do you see yourself in five, ten, or twenty years? This vision serves as the North Star that guides all of your subsequent goals.

Once you have a clear vision, you can break it down into smaller, more manageable goals. These can be short-term goals, such as launching a new product or increasing website traffic, or long-term goals, such as expanding into new markets or achieving a certain level of profitability. The key is to ensure that each goal is aligned with your overall vision and contributes to your ultimate success.

One of the most effective frameworks for goal setting is the SMART methodology. SMART goals are Specific, Measurable, Achievable, Relevant, and Time-bound. This approach ensures that your goals are well-defined, actionable, and realistic.

Specific: Your goals should be clear and concise, leaving no room for ambiguity. Instead of saying, "I want to increase sales," you might say, "I want to increase sales by 15% in the next quarter."

Measurable: Your goals should be quantifiable so that you can track your progress and determine whether you're on track to achieve them. This might involve setting key performance indicators (KPIs) or using other metrics to measure your success.

Achievable: Your goals should be challenging, but not so far-fetched that they become discouraging. It's important to set realistic goals that you can actually accomplish with the resources and time available to you.

Relevant: Your goals should be aligned with your overall vision and mission. They should be meaningful and contribute to your ultimate success.

Time-bound: Your goals should have a deadline or timeframe for completion. This creates a sense of urgency and helps you stay focused on achieving your objectives.

Setting SMART goals is just the first step. The next step is to create an action plan for achieving them. This involves breaking down each goal into smaller tasks or milestones and identifying the resources, skills, and support you need to succeed. It's also important to regularly review your goals and make adjustments as needed. Your goals are not set in stone; they should evolve as your business grows and circumstances change.

The benefits of goal setting for entrepreneurs are numerous. Goals can:

Increase motivation: When you have a clear target in mind, you're more likely to stay motivated and focused on achieving it.

Boost productivity: Goals provide a sense of direction and purpose, helping you prioritize tasks and make the most of your time.

Improve decision-making: When you know what you're working towards, you can make better decisions that align with your objectives.

Enhance focus: Goals help you avoid distractions and stay on track, even when faced with challenges or setbacks.

Foster resilience: When you encounter obstacles, having a clear goal in mind can help you stay motivated and persevere.

Measure progress: By tracking your progress towards your goals, you can identify areas where you're excelling and areas where you need to improve.

Celebrate success: Achieving your goals is a cause for celebration and can provide a sense of accomplishment and satisfaction.

In addition to the individual benefits, goal setting can also have a positive impact on your team and organization as a whole. When everyone is working towards a common set of goals, it creates a sense of unity and purpose. It can also improve communication, collaboration, and overall performance.

Goal setting is not a one-time event; it's an ongoing process. As an entrepreneur, you should continuously set new goals, revise existing ones, and adapt your strategies as needed. This will help you stay ahead of the curve, anticipate challenges, and seize new opportunities.

In conclusion, goal setting is not just a good practice for entrepreneurs; it's an essential one. It's the compass that guides your journey, ensuring that your efforts are aligned with your vision and ultimately, leading to your success. By setting clear, measurable, achievable, relevant, and time-bound goals, you can unlock your full potential, achieve your dreams, and make a lasting impact on the world.

ppp

Goals are the compass that guides your entrepreneurial journey. Set them with clarity, pursue them with passion, and celebrate every milestone along the way. Your destination awaits.

THREE

PRIORITIZATION: THE ART OF DOING LESS, BUT ACHIEVING MORE.

In the entrepreneurial world, where opportunities are abundant and time is a precious commodity, the ability to prioritize effectively can be the difference between thriving and merely surviving. It's a paradox that many entrepreneurs grapple with: the more successful they become, the more demands are placed on their time. The influx of emails, meetings, phone calls, and urgent tasks can quickly overwhelm even the most organized individual. This is where the art of prioritization comes into play.

Prioritization is not simply about creating a to-do list and checking off items in order. It's a strategic approach to managing your workload that involves identifying the most important tasks, focusing your energy on them, and delegating or eliminating the rest. The goal is to achieve more by doing less, to maximize your impact by concentrating on activities that truly move the needle.

The Pareto Principle, also known as the 80/20 rule, is a fundamental concept in prioritization. It states that roughly 80% of your results come from 20% of your efforts. This means that a small number of tasks are disproportionately responsible for your success. By identifying and focusing on these high-impact activities, you can significantly increase your productivity and effectiveness.

But how do you determine which tasks fall into that crucial 20%? This is where prioritization frameworks come in handy. There are numerous approaches to prioritization, each with its strengths and weaknesses. Some popular methods include:

The Eisenhower Matrix: This framework categorizes tasks into four quadrants based on their urgency and importance.

The ABCDE Method: This method ranks tasks from A (most important) to E (least important).

The MIT (Most Important Tasks) Method: This approach involves identifying the three most important tasks for the day and focusing on completing them first.

The Covey Time Management Matrix: This matrix categorizes tasks into four quadrants based on their urgency and importance, similar to the Eisenhower Matrix.

Regardless of the specific framework you choose, the underlying principle is the same: focus on the tasks that will have the biggest impact on your goals. This requires a deep understanding of your business, your priorities, and your strengths. It also involves the ability to say "no" to non-essential tasks, delegate effectively, and embrace the power of automation.

One of the most common mistakes entrepreneurs make is trying to do everything themselves. They believe that they're the only ones who can do certain tasks to their standards or that delegating will take more time than simply doing it themselves. However, this mindset can quickly lead to burnout and overwhelm. By learning to delegate or outsource tasks that are not in their zone of genius, entrepreneurs can free up valuable time to focus on activities that truly require their expertise.

Another common pitfall is getting bogged down in the minutiae of daily tasks. It's easy to become consumed by emails, meetings, and other urgent but not necessarily important activities. This is where time blocking can be a game-changer. By scheduling specific blocks of time for different types of tasks, you can ensure that you're dedicating adequate time to your most important priorities.

Prioritization is not a one-size-fits-all proposition. It's an ongoing process that requires constant evaluation and adjustment. As your business grows and evolves, so too will your priorities. It's important to regularly review your goals, assess your progress, and realign your efforts as needed.

In addition to the practical benefits of increased productivity and efficiency, prioritization can also have a profound impact on your well-being. When you're focused on meaningful work, you're more likely to experience a sense of purpose, fulfillment, and satisfaction. You're also less likely to feel stressed and overwhelmed.

The art of prioritization is not simply about getting more done; it's about achieving more with less effort. It's about working smarter, not harder. It's about focusing on what truly matters and letting go of the rest. By mastering this skill, entrepreneurs can unlock their full potential, achieve their goals, and create a business and life that they love.

In the grand scheme of entrepreneurship, prioritization is not just a tool; it's a philosophy. It's a mindset that embraces the power of focus, the importance of delegation, and the beauty of simplicity. It's a commitment to doing less, but achieving more. By embracing this philosophy, entrepreneurs can escape the trap of busyness, reclaim their time, and create a more meaningful and impactful life.

ᗧᗧᗧ

Don't be a slave to your to-do list. Prioritize ruthlessly, focus on high-impact activities, and delegate the rest. Remember, doing less can often lead to achieving more.

FOUR

Time Blocking: Structure Your Day for Maximum Efficiency.

In the bustling world of entrepreneurship, where distractions lurk around every corner and the to-do list seems to grow exponentially, mastering the art of time management is essential for achieving peak productivity and efficiency. One of the most effective strategies for taming the chaos and maximizing your output is time blocking. It's a simple yet powerful technique that involves dividing your day into specific blocks of time, each dedicated to a particular task or activity.

At its core, time blocking is about taking control of your schedule instead of letting it control you. It's about proactively planning your day rather than reactively responding to whatever comes your way. By allocating specific time slots for different tasks, you create a structured framework that eliminates the guesswork and ensures that your most important priorities get the attention they deserve.

The beauty of time blocking lies in its adaptability. It can be tailored to fit your unique work style, preferences, and energy levels. Some entrepreneurs prefer to schedule their most demanding tasks during their peak productivity hours, while others find it helpful to alternate between different types of activities to prevent burnout. The key is to experiment and find a rhythm that works best for you.

To get started with time blocking, begin by identifying your most important tasks for the day. These are the activities that directly contribute to your goals and have the biggest impact on your success. Once you have a clear understanding of your priorities, assign specific time blocks to each task. Be realistic about how long each task will take, and leave some buffer time for unexpected interruptions or delays.

One of the most effective ways to implement time blocking is to use a calendar or scheduling app. This allows you to visualize your day and easily adjust your schedule as needed. You can also use color-coding or other visual cues to differentiate between different types of tasks or activities.

When scheduling your time blocks, consider your energy levels throughout the day. Most people experience peaks and valleys in their energy and focus. By aligning your tasks with your natural rhythms, you can optimize your productivity and avoid burnout. For example, if you're most alert in the morning, schedule your most challenging tasks for that time. If you tend to experience a mid-afternoon slump, use that time for less demanding activities like checking emails or returning phone calls.

Another important aspect of time blocking is protecting your time. Once you've scheduled a block of time for a specific task, treat it as a non-negotiable appointment. Avoid distractions like social media, email, or unnecessary meetings. If possible, let your colleagues or team members know that you're unavailable during that time.

While time blocking can be a highly effective tool, it's not without its challenges. One common obstacle is the tendency to overestimate how much you can accomplish in a given time frame. It's important to be realistic about your capabilities and avoid overcommitting yourself. If you find that you're consistently running out of time, adjust your schedule accordingly.

Another challenge is dealing with unexpected interruptions or emergencies. While it's impossible to eliminate all disruptions, you can minimize their impact by building buffer time into your schedule. You can also use techniques like the Pomodoro Technique, which involves working in focused intervals with short breaks in between, to help you stay on track.

The benefits of time blocking for entrepreneurs are numerous. It can help you:

Increase Productivity: By focusing on one task at a time, you can eliminate distractions and achieve a state of flow, where you're fully immersed in your work and producing your best results.

Improve Focus: By scheduling specific time blocks for different activities, you can train your brain to focus on the task at hand and avoid multitasking, which has been shown to decrease productivity.

Reduce Stress: By having a clear plan for your day, you can reduce the anxiety and overwhelm that often comes with an overflowing to-do list.

Achieve Better Work-Life Balance: By scheduling time for both work and personal activities, you can create a more balanced and fulfilling life.

Gain a Sense of Accomplishment: By completing tasks within their designated time blocks, you can experience a sense of progress and accomplishment, which can boost your motivation and confidence.

Time blocking is not a magic bullet, but it's a powerful tool that can help you take control of your time, maximize your productivity, and achieve your goals. By incorporating it into your daily routine, you can transform the way you work and live, creating a more focused, efficient, and fulfilling entrepreneurial journey.

As with any new habit, implementing time blocking may take some time and effort. But with practice and persistence, it can become second nature, allowing you to harness the full potential of your time and unlock your true entrepreneurial potential. So, start today. Take a few minutes to plan your day, block out your time, and watch your productivity soar.

ᗺᗺᗺ

Structure your day with intention. Time block your schedule, batch similar tasks, and work when your energy is at its peak. A well-orchestrated day is a productive day.

FIVE

Task Batching: Group Similar Activities for Seamless Flow.

In the fast-paced world of entrepreneurship, efficiency is key. Every minute counts, and optimizing your workflow can make a significant difference in your productivity and overall success. One often overlooked strategy for achieving this is task batching. It's a simple yet powerful technique that involves grouping similar tasks together and completing them in one focused session. This approach not only streamlines your workflow but also enhances your focus, reduces mental fatigue, and ultimately saves you valuable time.

The concept of task batching is rooted in the idea of context switching. When you constantly switch between different types of tasks, your brain has to reorient itself each time, which takes time and energy. This constant shifting of gears can lead to mental fatigue, decreased productivity, and increased errors. Task batching eliminates this problem by allowing you to focus on one type of activity at a time, minimizing context switching and maximizing your efficiency.

Think of it like cooking a meal. Instead of jumping back and forth between chopping vegetables, boiling pasta, and preheating the oven, you would typically complete each task in sequence. You would chop all the vegetables at once, then boil the pasta, and finally preheat the oven. This approach is more efficient because it eliminates the need to constantly switch between different tools and ingredients.

The same principle applies to your work. By batching similar tasks together, you can create a streamlined workflow that allows you to move seamlessly from one task to the next without losing momentum. For example, instead of responding to emails sporadically throughout the day, you could set aside a specific time block to process all of your emails at once. This would eliminate the constant interruptions and allow you to focus on the task at hand.

Another example of task batching is content creation. Instead of writing one blog post at a time, you could batch your writing by outlining several posts in one session, drafting them in another, and editing them in a third. This approach allows you to get into a writing flow state and produce high-quality content more efficiently.

The benefits of task batching are numerous. It can:

Increase Productivity: By minimizing context switching and allowing you to focus on one type of task at a time, task batching can significantly increase your productivity. You'll be able to complete tasks more quickly and with fewer errors.

Enhance Focus: When you're not constantly switching between

different tasks, you can more easily enter a state of flow, where you're fully immersed in your work and producing your best results.

Reduce Mental Fatigue: Context switching can be mentally taxing. By batching tasks, you can reduce the cognitive load on your brain and avoid burnout.

Save Time: By eliminating the need to constantly switch gears, task batching can save you valuable time. You'll be able to complete more tasks in less time.

Improve Organization: By grouping similar tasks together, you can create a more organized and streamlined workflow. This can make it easier to track your progress and ensure that nothing falls through the cracks.

To get started with task batching, begin by identifying the types of tasks that you regularly perform. These could include emails, meetings, phone calls, content creation, administrative tasks, or any other activity that you find yourself doing repeatedly. Once you've identified your tasks, group them into categories based on their similarity. For example, you could group all of your email-related tasks together, all of your content creation tasks together, and so on.

Next, schedule specific time blocks for each category of tasks. The length of each time block will depend on the nature of the tasks and your personal preferences. Some tasks may only require a short burst of focus, while others may need a longer, uninterrupted period of time.

Once you've scheduled your time blocks, stick to your schedule as closely as possible. Of course, there will be times when unexpected events arise, but try to minimize interruptions and distractions as much as possible. When you're in a task batching session, focus solely on the tasks in that category. Avoid checking email, social media, or other distractions that can pull you out of your flow state.

Task batching is a versatile technique that can be applied to a wide range of activities. It's particularly well-suited for tasks that require similar mental processes or tools. However, it can also be used for tasks that are simply time-consuming or repetitive. By grouping these tasks together, you can get them out of the way quickly and efficiently, freeing up your time for more important or creative work.

Task batching is a simple yet effective strategy for maximizing your productivity and efficiency. By grouping similar tasks together and completing them in focused sessions, you can minimize context switching, enhance your focus, reduce mental fatigue, and ultimately save valuable time. Whether you're an entrepreneur, a freelancer, or a busy professional, task batching can help you streamline your workflow and achieve your goals. So, why not give it a try? You may be surprised at how much more you can accomplish in less time.

▷▷▷

Your energy is your fuel. Nourish it with rest, exercise, and healthy habits. A well-rested entrepreneur is a creative and resilient one.

SIX

ENERGY MANAGEMENT: WORK WHEN YOU'RE MOST PRODUCTIVE.

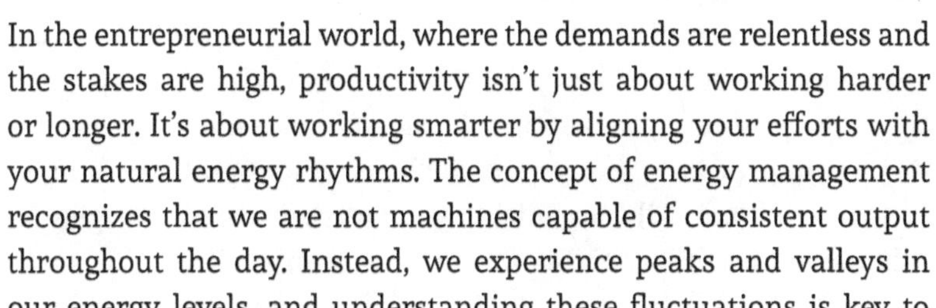

In the entrepreneurial world, where the demands are relentless and the stakes are high, productivity isn't just about working harder or longer. It's about working smarter by aligning your efforts with your natural energy rhythms. The concept of energy management recognizes that we are not machines capable of consistent output throughout the day. Instead, we experience peaks and valleys in our energy levels, and understanding these fluctuations is key to optimizing our performance.

Traditional time management often focuses on rigidly scheduling tasks and activities, regardless of our energy levels. However, this approach can lead to burnout, frustration, and ultimately, decreased productivity. Energy management, on the other hand, encourages us to work in harmony with our natural energy cycles, maximizing our output during peak periods and resting or engaging in less demanding tasks during lulls.

Our energy levels are influenced by a variety of factors, including our sleep patterns, diet, exercise habits, and even our emotional state. To effectively manage our energy, we must first become aware of our own unique rhythms. This involves paying attention to when we feel most alert, focused, and creative, as well as when we feel sluggish, distracted, or unmotivated. By tracking our energy levels throughout the day, we can begin to identify patterns and adjust our schedules accordingly.

For most people, energy levels tend to be highest in the morning, after a good night's sleep and a nutritious breakfast. This is often the ideal time to tackle your most challenging and important tasks, the ones that require deep focus and concentration. By prioritizing these activities during your peak energy hours, you can leverage your natural alertness and cognitive abilities to achieve optimal results.

As the day progresses, energy levels typically begin to decline. This is a natural part of our circadian rhythm, the internal clock that regulates our sleep-wake cycle. During these lulls, it's important to avoid pushing yourself too hard and instead focus on less demanding tasks. This could include responding to emails, returning phone calls, organizing your workspace, or engaging in other activities that don't require as much mental effort.

By respecting your natural energy rhythms, you can avoid burnout and maintain a high level of productivity throughout the day. Instead of forcing yourself to work when you're feeling drained, take a break, go for a walk, or engage in a relaxing activity. This will allow you to recharge your batteries and return to your work with renewed focus and energy.

In addition to aligning your tasks with your energy levels, there are other strategies you can employ to optimize your performance. For example, you can:

Prioritize Sleep: Getting enough sleep is essential for maintaining optimal energy levels. Aim for 7-8 hours of sleep per night and establish a regular sleep schedule.

Eat a Healthy Diet: Fuel your body with nutritious foods that provide sustained energy throughout the day. Avoid sugary drinks and processed foods, which can lead to energy crashes.

Exercise Regularly: Exercise can boost your energy levels, improve your mood, and enhance your cognitive function. Aim for at least 30 minutes of moderate-intensity exercise most days of the week.

Manage Stress: Stress can drain your energy and negatively impact your productivity. Find healthy ways to manage stress, such as meditation, yoga, or spending time in nature.

Take Breaks: Don't try to work for hours on end without taking breaks. Get up and move around, step outside for fresh air, or simply close your eyes and rest for a few minutes.

Delegate Tasks: If you're feeling overwhelmed, don't be afraid to delegate tasks to others. This will free up your time and energy for the tasks that require your personal attention.

By implementing these strategies, you can create a sustainable approach to energy management that will help you maintain high levels of productivity and well-being over the long term. Remember, energy management is not about pushing yourself to the limit; it's about working smarter, not harder. By understanding your own unique energy rhythms and aligning your tasks accordingly, you can achieve more with less effort and create a more fulfilling and sustainable entrepreneurial journey.

It's also important to note that energy management is not just about maximizing your productivity; it's also about protecting your health and well-being. When you consistently push yourself beyond your limits, you risk burnout, which can lead to physical and emotional exhaustion, decreased motivation, and even health problems. By prioritizing your energy management, you're investing in your long-term health and success.

Energy management is a powerful tool that can help entrepreneurs unlock their full potential. By understanding their natural energy rhythms and aligning their tasks accordingly, they can maximize their productivity, reduce stress, and achieve a more fulfilling and sustainable work-life balance. So, if you're an entrepreneur looking to take your productivity to the next level, start paying attention to your energy levels. Experiment with different strategies and find what works best for you. Remember, it's not about working harder; it's about working smarter.

ϸϸϸ

Procrastination is the thief of time. Embrace the Pomodoro Technique, break down tasks into manageable chunks, and conquer the urge to delay.

SEVEN

THE POMODORO TECHNIQUE: CONQUER PROCRASTINATION WITH FOCUSED INTERVALS.

Procrastination, the arch-nemesis of productivity, is a universal struggle that plagues entrepreneurs and professionals alike. It's that insidious force that lures us into postponing important tasks in favor of less urgent or more enjoyable activities. While the allure of instant gratification may be tempting in the moment, the consequences of procrastination can be severe, leading to missed deadlines, increased stress, and a sense of overwhelm. Fortunately, there's a simple yet effective technique that can help you conquer procrastination and regain control of your time: the Pomodoro Technique.

The Pomodoro Technique is a time management method developed by Francesco Cirillo in the late 1980s. It's a structured approach that involves breaking down work into intervals, traditionally 25 minutes in length, separated by short breaks. These intervals are called "pomodoros," named after the tomato-shaped kitchen timer Cirillo used to track his work sessions.

The core principle of the Pomodoro Technique is to focus on one task at a time for a set period, then take a short break to rest and recharge. This cycle of focused work followed by short breaks helps to maintain your energy levels, prevent burnout, and improve your overall productivity. It also helps to reduce distractions and procrastination by creating a sense of urgency and accountability.

To get started with the Pomodoro Technique, you'll need a timer, a to-do list, and a pen and paper or a digital note-taking app. Begin by choosing a task that you want to work on. Set your timer for 25 minutes and work on the task with full concentration, avoiding any distractions. When the timer goes off, take a five-minute break. During your break, get up and move around, stretch, grab a drink of water, or do something else that will help you relax and recharge.

After four pomodoros, take a longer break of 20-30 minutes. This longer break is important for giving your brain a chance to fully rest and reset. During this break, you can go for a walk, listen to music, meditate, or engage in any other activity that will help you de-stress and recharge.

The Pomodoro Technique is incredibly flexible and can be adapted to fit your individual needs and preferences. You can adjust the length of your work intervals and breaks, change the number of pomodoros you complete in a row, or even combine the technique with other time management methods. The key is to find a rhythm that works for you and stick with it.

One of the biggest benefits of the Pomodoro Technique is its ability to combat procrastination. By breaking down large tasks into smaller, more manageable chunks, it makes them seem less daunting and more achievable. The timer also creates a sense of urgency and accountability, which can help you overcome the temptation to procrastinate.

Another advantage of the Pomodoro Technique is its ability to improve focus and concentration. When you know you only have 25 minutes to work on a task, you're more likely to eliminate distractions and focus on the task at hand. The short breaks also help to prevent mental fatigue and maintain your energy levels throughout the day.

The Pomodoro Technique can also be a valuable tool for managing time and increasing productivity. By tracking your pomodoros, you can gain a better understanding of how long it takes you to complete different types of tasks. This information can help you plan your work more effectively and set realistic goals.

Additionally, the Pomodoro Technique can help you develop a more sustainable work routine. By working in short bursts with regular breaks, you can avoid burnout and maintain your productivity over the long term. This is especially important for entrepreneurs, who often work long hours and face intense pressure.

While the Pomodoro Technique is a simple and effective method, it's not without its challenges. One common obstacle is the temptation to interrupt your work intervals. It's easy to get distracted by emails, phone calls, or other urgent tasks. However, it's important to resist these distractions and stick to your schedule. If something truly urgent arises, deal with it quickly and then return to your pomodoro.

Another challenge is finding the right balance between work and breaks. Some people find that 25-minute work intervals are too short, while others find them too long. It's important to experiment and find a rhythm that works for you. If you're struggling to focus for 25 minutes, try shortening your intervals to 15 or 20 minutes. If you're feeling restless during your breaks, try extending them to 10 or 15 minutes.

The Pomodoro Technique is not a magic bullet, but it's a valuable tool that can help you overcome procrastination, improve your focus, and boost your productivity. It's a simple yet effective method that can be easily incorporated into your daily routine. By embracing the Pomodoro Technique, you can take control of your time, achieve your goals, and live a more productive and fulfilling life.

ᗞᗞᗞ

The 80/20 rule is your secret weapon. Identify the 20% of tasks that drive 80% of your results and focus your energy there. This is where the magic happens.

EIGHT

THE 80/20 RULE: IDENTIFY THE TASKS THAT DRIVE 80% OF YOUR RESULTS.

In the fast-paced and often chaotic world of entrepreneurship, where time is a precious commodity and demands are endless, maximizing efficiency and productivity is paramount. The 80/20 Rule, also known as the Pareto Principle, offers a powerful framework for achieving this goal. This principle, named after Italian economist Vilfredo Pareto, posits that roughly 80% of outcomes result from 20% of causes. In the context of business and entrepreneurship, this translates to the idea that a small fraction of your efforts and activities generate the majority of your results.

The 80/20 Rule is a universal principle that applies to a wide range of phenomena. For example, in sales, 20% of your customers may account for 80% of your revenue. In software development, 20% of the code may cause 80% of the errors. In your personal life, 20% of your relationships may bring you 80% of your happiness. By recognizing this pattern, you can identify the most impactful areas to focus your energy and resources, leading to exponential growth and success.

For entrepreneurs, the 80/20 Rule is a game-changer. It challenges the traditional notion that all tasks are created equal and encourages a shift in mindset towards prioritizing high-impact activities. By identifying the 20% of tasks that drive 80% of your results, you can streamline your workflow, eliminate time-wasting activities, and achieve more with less effort.

Applying the 80/20 Rule in your entrepreneurial endeavors requires a systematic approach. First, you need to identify the key areas of your business that are most critical to your success. This could include product development, marketing and sales, customer service, or financial management. Once you've identified these areas, you need to analyze your activities within each area to determine which ones are generating the most significant results.

This analysis can be done through various methods, such as tracking your time, analyzing your sales data, or soliciting feedback from customers. The goal is to gain a clear understanding of where your efforts are yielding the greatest return on investment. Once you've identified your high-impact activities, you can then focus your time and resources on these areas, while delegating or eliminating the rest.

The benefits of applying the 80/20 Rule to your entrepreneurial ventures are manifold. It can help you:

Increase Productivity: By focusing on high-impact activities, you can achieve more in less time, leading to increased productivity and efficiency.

Improve Focus: By eliminating time-wasting activities, you can sharpen your focus and concentrate on the tasks that truly matter.

Reduce Stress: By prioritizing your workload and delegating non-essential tasks, you can reduce stress and overwhelm.

Maximize Profits: By focusing on the 20% of customers or products that generate 80% of your revenue, you can optimize your profitability.

Enhance Decision-Making: By understanding which activities are most impactful, you can make more informed decisions about where to allocate your resources.

The 80/20 Rule is not a one-size-fits-all solution, and its application will vary depending on your specific business and industry. However, the underlying principle remains the same: focus on the few activities that generate the most significant results. This requires a willingness to challenge conventional wisdom, let go of unproductive habits, and embrace a more strategic approach to your work.

In addition to applying the 80/20 Rule to your business operations, you can also use it to optimize your personal life. For example, you can identify the 20% of your relationships that bring you the most joy and fulfillment and invest more time and energy in those relationships. You can also identify the 20% of your hobbies or activities that bring you the most satisfaction and prioritize those activities over others.

By applying the 80/20 Rule to both your professional and personal life, you can create a more balanced and fulfilling lifestyle. You can achieve more with less effort, reduce stress, and focus on the activities and relationships that truly matter.

The 80/20 Rule is a powerful tool that can help entrepreneurs maximize their productivity, efficiency, and overall success. By identifying the tasks that drive 80% of your results and focusing your energy on those activities, you can streamline your workflow, eliminate time-wasting activities, and achieve more with less effort. The 80/20 Rule is not just a principle; it's a mindset. It's about working smarter, not harder. It's about focusing on what truly matters and letting go of the rest. By embracing this mindset, you can unlock your full potential and achieve your entrepreneurial dreams.

ϷϷϷ

Don't try to be a superhero. Delegate tasks, outsource expertise, and leverage the power of others. Building a strong team is key to entrepreneurial success.

NINE

DELEGATION & OUTSOURCING: LEVERAGE THE POWER OF OTHERS.

In the entrepreneurial journey, the desire to maintain control and handle every aspect of the business is a common instinct. After all, it's your vision, your passion project. However, as the business grows and responsibilities multiply, the limitations of this approach become apparent. The entrepreneurial spirit that drove you to launch your venture can easily become stifled by the weight of endless tasks. This is where the power of delegation and outsourcing comes into play.

Delegation and outsourcing are not signs of weakness or a lack of capability. Instead, they are strategic tools that can empower entrepreneurs to focus on their core strengths, accelerate growth, and achieve a healthier work-life balance. By leveraging the skills and expertise of others, you can free yourself from the shackles of micromanagement and create a more sustainable and scalable business model.

Delegation involves entrusting tasks or responsibilities to someone else within your organization, typically an employee or team member. It's about recognizing that you can't do everything yourself and that empowering others can lead to greater efficiency and productivity. When done effectively, delegation fosters trust, builds morale, and develops the skills of your team. It also allows you to focus on higher-level tasks that require your unique expertise and vision.

Outsourcing, on the other hand, involves contracting external individuals or companies to perform specific tasks or functions. This can be a cost-effective way to access specialized skills and expertise that may not be available in-house. Outsourcing can also help you scale your business more quickly by providing access to a wider range of resources and capabilities.

The decision to delegate or outsource should be based on a careful analysis of your business needs, budget, and available resources. Some tasks may be better suited for delegation, while others may be more effectively handled by outsourcing. For example, routine administrative tasks or customer support may be easily delegated to employees, while specialized tasks like web development or graphic design may be better outsourced to experts.

When deciding which tasks to delegate or outsource, it's important to consider your core competencies. These are the skills and activities that you excel at and that are essential to the success of your business. By focusing on your core competencies and delegating or outsourcing the rest, you can maximize your impact and achieve greater results.

Delegation and outsourcing can also help you overcome the limitations of time and resources. As an entrepreneur, you have a finite amount of time and energy. By delegating or outsourcing tasks that are not essential to your core competencies, you can free up valuable time to focus on strategic initiatives, innovation, and growth.

Effective delegation and outsourcing require careful planning and execution. It's not simply about handing off tasks and hoping for the best. You need to clearly define the scope of work, set expectations, provide adequate resources and support, and establish a system for monitoring progress and providing feedback.

One of the most common challenges in delegation is the fear of losing control. Entrepreneurs often feel that they need to be involved in every aspect of their business to ensure that things are done right. However, this mindset can lead to micromanagement, which can stifle creativity, demoralize employees, and hinder growth.

To overcome this fear, it's important to trust your team and empower them to take ownership of their responsibilities. This involves providing clear instructions, setting realistic expectations, and providing ongoing support and guidance. It also involves recognizing that mistakes are a natural part of the learning process and that they can provide valuable opportunities for growth.

Another challenge in outsourcing is finding the right partners. Not all outsourcing providers are created equal, and it's important to do your due diligence before selecting a partner. This involves researching their reputation, reviewing their portfolio, and getting references from other clients. It's also important to clearly define your expectations and ensure that the provider has the skills and resources to meet your needs.

When done effectively, delegation and outsourcing can be powerful tools for accelerating growth, improving efficiency, and achieving a healthier work-life balance. By leveraging the skills and expertise of others, you can free yourself from the shackles of micromanagement, focus on your core competencies, and create a more sustainable and scalable business model.

❧❧❧

Embrace the power of automation. Let technology handle the mundane, repetitive tasks so you can focus on what truly matters: growing your business.

TEN

Automation: Harness Technology to Streamline Repetitive Tasks.

In the ever-evolving landscape of entrepreneurship, time is an invaluable asset. The ability to optimize workflows and maximize efficiency is paramount to achieving success in today's fast-paced business environment. A key strategy for unlocking these benefits is through automation. Automation refers to the use of technology to perform tasks that were once done manually, allowing entrepreneurs to streamline repetitive processes, reduce human error, and free up valuable time for more strategic initiatives.

The impact of automation on business operations is undeniable. By automating repetitive tasks, entrepreneurs can significantly enhance productivity and efficiency. For example, instead of manually entering data into spreadsheets, businesses can utilize automation tools to extract and process information from various sources, saving countless hours of manual labor. This not only reduces the risk of errors but also allows employees to focus on more complex and value-added activities.

The benefits of automation extend beyond increased productivity. By automating mundane and repetitive tasks, businesses can improve employee morale and job satisfaction. Employees are freed from the monotony of repetitive work and can instead focus on more challenging and engaging projects. This can lead to increased creativity, innovation, and overall job satisfaction.

Automation can also significantly reduce operational costs. By automating tasks that were once performed by humans, businesses can save on labor costs, reduce the need for overtime, and minimize the risk of errors that can lead to costly rework or customer dissatisfaction. Additionally, automation can help businesses optimize their resource allocation, ensuring that resources are used efficiently and effectively.

The applications of automation in business are vast and varied. In marketing, automation tools can be used to personalize email campaigns, schedule social media posts, and track customer engagement. In sales, automation can streamline lead generation, automate follow-up processes, and personalize customer interactions. In customer service, automation can be used to handle routine inquiries, route complex issues to the appropriate agents, and provide 24/7 support.

Even in back-office operations like finance and accounting, automation can play a crucial role. Tasks like invoicing, expense tracking, and payroll processing can be automated, saving valuable time and reducing the risk of errors. Furthermore, automation can help businesses gain valuable insights into their operations by providing real-time data and analytics. By tracking key performance indicators (KPIs) and identifying trends, businesses can make data-driven decisions and continuously improve their processes.

One of the most exciting aspects of automation is its potential to transform the way we work. As technology continues to advance, we can expect to see even more sophisticated automation tools that can handle increasingly complex tasks. This has the potential to revolutionize industries, create new job opportunities, and reshape the global economy.

However, the rise of automation also raises important questions about the future of work and the role of humans in the workplace. As machines become more capable of performing tasks that were once thought to be exclusively human, there are concerns about job displacement and the need for reskilling and upskilling. While automation may eliminate certain jobs, it is also expected to create new ones, particularly in fields that require creativity, critical thinking, and interpersonal skills.

To thrive in the age of automation, entrepreneurs and businesses must embrace a mindset of continuous learning and adaptability. By investing in new skills and technologies, they can stay ahead of the curve and leverage automation to their advantage. This may involve training employees on how to use automation tools, partnering with technology providers, or even developing their own custom solutions.

The key to successful automation is to strike a balance between human and machine capabilities. While automation can handle repetitive and rule-based tasks, humans excel at creativity, problem-solving, and decision-making. By combining the strengths of both, businesses can achieve optimal results.

In conclusion, automation is a powerful tool that can transform the way entrepreneurs and businesses operate. By streamlining repetitive tasks, reducing costs, and improving efficiency, automation can unlock new levels of productivity and success. However, it's important to approach automation strategically and to ensure that it is used in a way that complements and enhances human capabilities. By embracing automation as a tool for innovation and growth, entrepreneurs can position themselves for success in the digital age.

ᚦᚦᚦ

"No" is a complete sentence. Protect your time from non-essential commitments. Learn to say "no" with grace and confidence.

ELEVEN

Saying "No": Protect Your Time from Non-Essential Commitments.

In the entrepreneurial arena, opportunities abound. It's a world filled with potential partnerships, collaborations, speaking engagements, networking events, and countless other possibilities. Saying "yes" to every opportunity that comes your way may seem like the path to success. However, this indiscriminate acceptance can quickly lead to overwhelm, burnout, and a dilution of your focus. To truly thrive as an entrepreneur, it's crucial to master the art of saying "no" and protecting your time from non-essential commitments.

Time is the most valuable asset an entrepreneur possesses. It's finite, irreplaceable, and directly impacts your ability to achieve your goals. When you say "yes" to everything, you're essentially giving away pieces of your most precious resource. This can lead to a fragmented schedule, reduced productivity, and a lack of progress on your most important priorities.

Saying "no" is not about being negative or uncooperative. It's about being strategic and intentional with your time. It's about recognizing that every commitment you make comes at a cost, and that cost is your time. By carefully evaluating each opportunity and saying "no" to those that don't align with your goals or priorities, you can safeguard your time and ensure that you're investing it in activities that will truly move the needle.

The fear of missing out (FOMO) is a common obstacle to saying "no." Entrepreneurs often worry that declining an opportunity will lead to missed connections, potential clients, or valuable experiences. While it's true that some opportunities may be beneficial, it's equally important to recognize that not all opportunities are created equal. Some may be distractions that take you off course, while others may simply not be the right fit for your business at this time.

To overcome the fear of missing out, it's important to have a clear understanding of your priorities and goals. What are the most important things you want to achieve with your business? What are your non-negotiables? Once you have a clear sense of your priorities, you can evaluate each opportunity against these criteria and make informed decisions about whether to say "yes" or "no."

Another common challenge to saying "no" is the desire to please others. Entrepreneurs often feel obligated to say "yes" to requests from friends, family, colleagues, or even strangers. However, it's important to remember that your time is valuable and that you have a right to protect it.

To overcome the desire to please others, it's important to practice assertiveness. This means expressing your needs and opinions in a clear and direct way, while still being respectful of others. It also means setting boundaries and communicating them clearly. For example, you might let people know that you only check emails at certain times of the day or that you're not available for meetings on certain days of the week.

Saying "no" doesn't have to be harsh or abrupt. There are many ways to decline an opportunity gracefully and tactfully. You can simply say, "Thank you for the opportunity, but I'm not able to commit to that at this time." You can also offer an alternative solution or suggest someone else who might be a better fit.

The key is to be honest and direct without being rude or dismissive. Remember, saying "no" is not a rejection of the person or the opportunity itself; it's simply a recognition that it's not the right fit for you at this time.

By mastering the art of saying "no," you can protect your time, maintain your focus, and achieve your entrepreneurial goals. It's a skill that requires practice and discipline, but the rewards are immeasurable. When you're able to say "no" with confidence and clarity, you'll find that you have more time and energy for the things that truly matter. You'll be able to focus on your most important priorities, build a thriving business, and create a life that you love.

Create a sanctuary for focus. Minimize distractions, declutter your workspace, and cultivate an environment that nurtures productivity.

TWELVE

Minimizing Distractions: Create a Focus-Friendly Environment.

In the modern world, distractions are ubiquitous. From the constant ping of notifications to the allure of social media, our attention is constantly being pulled in multiple directions. For entrepreneurs, this can be especially detrimental, as focus and concentration are essential for making progress on important tasks and achieving goals. Creating a focus-friendly environment is therefore crucial for maximizing productivity and minimizing the negative impact of distractions.

The first step in creating a focus-friendly environment is to identify your personal triggers. What are the things that most easily distract you? Is it email notifications, social media, phone calls, or something else? Once you know what your triggers are, you can start to implement strategies to minimize their impact.

One of the most effective ways to minimize distractions is to eliminate them altogether. This might mean turning off notifications on your phone or computer, closing unnecessary tabs in your browser, or finding a quiet workspace where you won't be interrupted. While it may not be possible to eliminate all distractions, every little bit helps.

If you can't eliminate distractions entirely, try to minimize them as much as possible. This might mean setting specific times for checking email or social media, using noise-canceling headphones to block out background noise, or simply letting your colleagues know that you're not available for interruptions.

Another important aspect of creating a focus-friendly environment is to declutter your workspace. A cluttered desk or office can be a major source of distraction. Take some time to tidy up your workspace and remove any unnecessary items. Keep only the essentials within reach and create a designated space for everything.

The physical environment also plays a role in your ability to focus. Make sure your workspace is well-lit, comfortable, and free of excessive noise. If possible, choose a workspace with a view of nature, as studies have shown that exposure to nature can improve focus and concentration.

Temperature can also affect your ability to focus. If you're too hot or too cold, you'll be more likely to get distracted. Make sure your workspace is at a comfortable temperature, and dress in layers so you can adjust as needed.

Another factor to consider is your posture. If you're slouching or hunching over your desk, you're more likely to experience fatigue and discomfort, which can lead to distractions. Make sure you're sitting up straight with your feet flat on the floor. You may also want to invest in an ergonomic chair or keyboard to ensure that your workspace is comfortable and supportive.

In addition to the physical environment, your mental state can also impact your ability to focus. If you're feeling stressed, anxious, or overwhelmed, it will be more difficult to concentrate on your work. Take some time to relax and de-stress before starting a task that requires focus. This might mean taking a few deep breaths, meditating, or listening to calming music.

It's also important to take breaks throughout the day. Our brains are not designed to focus for extended periods without rest. Taking short breaks can help you recharge your mental batteries and return to your work with renewed focus. Get up and move around, stretch, or step outside for some fresh air.

Another helpful strategy is to break down large tasks into smaller, more manageable chunks. This can make them seem less daunting and more achievable. Set realistic goals for each work session and celebrate your progress along the way.

Technology can be both a blessing and a curse when it comes to focus. While it can provide us with valuable tools and resources, it can also be a major source of distraction. To minimize the negative impact of technology, set boundaries for your use of electronic devices. This might mean turning off notifications, silencing your phone, or using website blockers to prevent you from accessing distracting websites.

Creating a focus-friendly environment is an ongoing process. It requires constant vigilance and a willingness to adapt as your needs and circumstances change. However, the effort is well worth it. By minimizing distractions and creating a space where you can focus on your work, you'll be more productive, efficient, and successful. You'll also experience less stress, greater well-being, and a deeper sense of satisfaction with your work.

In conclusion, minimizing distractions and creating a focus-friendly environment is essential for entrepreneurial success. By identifying your triggers, eliminating or minimizing distractions, decluttering your workspace, optimizing your physical environment, and managing your mental state, you can create a space where you can focus on your work and achieve your goals. Remember, focus is a skill that can be developed with practice and dedication. By making a conscious effort to create a focus-friendly environment, you can unlock your full potential and achieve your entrepreneurial dreams.

ᗡᗡᗡ

Time tracking is your mirror. It reflects how you're spending your most valuable asset. Analyze the data, identify time sinks, and optimize your schedule.

THIRTEEN

TIME TRACKING & ANALYSIS: UNDERSTAND WHERE YOUR TIME GOES.

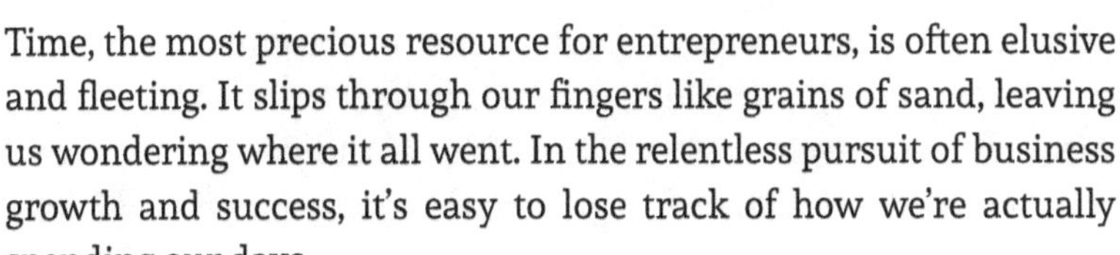

Time, the most precious resource for entrepreneurs, is often elusive and fleeting. It slips through our fingers like grains of sand, leaving us wondering where it all went. In the relentless pursuit of business growth and success, it's easy to lose track of how we're actually spending our days.

This is where time tracking and analysis become indispensable tools for gaining clarity, optimizing our schedules, and ultimately, achieving greater productivity and fulfillment.

Time tracking, at its core, is the practice of recording how much time you spend on different tasks and activities. It involves meticulously logging the minutes and hours dedicated to various aspects of your work, from meetings and emails to project work and client interactions.

This data, when analyzed, provides a treasure trove of insights into your work habits, time allocation, and overall efficiency.

The benefits of time tracking are manifold. First and foremost, it provides a reality check on how you're actually spending your time. We often have a skewed perception of our time allocation, overestimating the time spent on productive tasks and underestimating the time wasted on distractions.

Time tracking reveals the truth, exposing hidden time sinks and highlighting areas where we can improve.

Moreover, time tracking helps identify patterns and trends in your work habits. Are you spending too much time on meetings? Are you getting bogged down in emails? Are you dedicating enough time to your most important projects? By analyzing your time tracking data, you can pinpoint these patterns and make necessary adjustments to optimize your schedule.

Time tracking also fosters a greater sense of accountability. When you know that you're being tracked, you're more likely to stay focused and avoid distractions. It's a subtle yet powerful psychological effect that can significantly boost your productivity.

Additionally, time tracking can help you identify your peak performance times. Are you more productive in the morning, afternoon, or evening? By understanding your natural rhythms, you can schedule your most demanding tasks for when you're most alert and focused.

Once you've collected sufficient time tracking data, the next step is analysis. This involves reviewing your logs and extracting meaningful insights. You can categorize your activities, calculate the average time spent on each task, and identify trends over time.

This analysis can reveal valuable information, such as which tasks are taking up the most time, which ones are most productive, and which ones can be delegated or eliminated.

There are various tools and methods for time tracking and analysis. Traditional methods include using a pen and paper or a spreadsheet to manually log your activities. However, with the advent of technology, numerous time tracking apps and software have emerged, making the process more convenient and efficient.

These tools often offer features like automatic time tracking, customizable reports, and integrations with other productivity apps.

When choosing a time tracking tool, consider your specific needs and preferences. Some tools are designed for individual use, while others are more suitable for teams. Some offer basic time tracking features, while others provide more advanced analytics and reporting capabilities. Choose a tool that fits your workflow and budget.

Regardless of the tool you choose, the key to successful time tracking is consistency. Make it a habit to track your time every day, even if it's just for a few minutes. The more data you collect, the more accurate and insightful your analysis will be.

Time tracking is not a one-time activity; it's an ongoing process. As your business evolves and your priorities change, so too will your time allocation. Regularly review your time tracking data and make adjustments as needed to ensure that you're always working on your most important tasks.

Time tracking and analysis are essential tools for entrepreneurs who want to take control of their time and maximize their productivity. By understanding where your time goes, you can identify inefficiencies, eliminate time-wasters, and focus on activities that truly move the needle.

It's a simple yet powerful practice that can have a profound impact on your business and your life. So, start tracking your time today and discover the hidden potential within your schedule.

ﭖﭖﭖ

Meetings don't have to be a waste of time. Set clear goals, create agendas, invite the right people, and use technology effectively. Make every meeting count.

FOURTEEN

MEETING MASTERY: MAKE MEETINGS PRODUCTIVE AND EFFICIENT.

In the fast-paced world of entrepreneurship, time is a precious commodity. Every minute spent on unproductive activities is a minute lost that could have been invested in growing your business, fostering innovation, or simply enjoying personal time. Yet, meetings, a seemingly indispensable part of the corporate world, have earned a notorious reputation for being time-wasters, productivity killers, and morale drainers. However, with the right approach and strategies, meetings can be transformed into powerful tools for collaboration, decision-making, and progress.

The first step in mastering the art of productive meetings is to question the necessity of a meeting in the first place. Before scheduling a meeting, ask yourself if the desired outcome can be achieved through alternative means, such as a quick email exchange, a phone call, or a shared document. If a meeting is indeed necessary, then it's crucial to define its purpose clearly. What are you hoping to achieve? What are the key decisions that need to be made? What information needs to be shared? By establishing a clear purpose, you can ensure that the meeting stays focused and on track.

An agenda is the backbone of a productive meeting. It outlines the topics to be discussed, the time allotted for each topic, and the desired outcomes. A well-crafted agenda sets expectations, keeps participants on track, and ensures that everyone is prepared. It's best to share the agenda in advance so that participants have time to review the materials and come prepared with questions or insights.

The success of a meeting hinges on the participation of the right people. Avoid inviting individuals who are not essential to the discussion or decision-making process. Too many participants can lead to distractions, tangential discussions, and ultimately, wasted time. Instead, invite only those who have a direct stake in the outcome or who can contribute valuable insights.

As the meeting organizer, your role is to facilitate the discussion and ensure that everyone has a chance to contribute. This involves setting ground rules, encouraging participation, and keeping the discussion focused. It's also important to manage time effectively, ensuring that each topic is given adequate attention but not allowed to drag on unnecessarily.

Technology can be a powerful tool for enhancing meeting productivity. Video conferencing platforms like Zoom or Microsoft Teams can enable virtual meetings, eliminating the need for travel and saving valuable time. Collaboration tools like Google Docs or Miro can facilitate real-time brainstorming and document sharing, while project management tools like Asana or Trello can help track action items and ensure accountability.

To maximize engagement and participation, consider incorporating interactive elements into your meetings. This could involve using polls or surveys to gather feedback, brainstorming sessions to generate ideas, or breakout groups to tackle specific issues. By actively involving participants, you can tap into their collective wisdom and creativity.

The end of a meeting is just as important as the beginning. Before adjourning, summarize the key takeaways, assign action items, and set clear deadlines. This ensures that everyone leaves the meeting with a clear understanding of what needs to be done and by when. It's also a good practice to send out meeting minutes summarizing the key points and action items as a reminder and reference for participants.

Feedback is a valuable tool for continuous improvement. After the meeting, solicit feedback from participants to gauge its effectiveness and identify areas for improvement. This can be done through anonymous surveys, one-on-one conversations, or even a dedicated feedback session. By actively seeking feedback and acting on it, you can continuously refine your meeting practices and ensure that they are as productive and efficient as possible.

While these strategies can significantly enhance meeting productivity, there are also some common pitfalls to avoid. One common mistake is failing to establish clear goals and objectives. Without a clear direction, meetings can easily devolve into aimless discussions that waste time and accomplish little.

Another common mistake is over-reliance on technology. While technology can be a powerful tool, it's important to use it judiciously. Technical glitches, distractions from notifications, and the impersonal nature of virtual meetings can all hinder productivity. Strive for a balance between technology and human interaction to ensure that your meetings are both efficient and engaging.

Finally, it's important to remember that meetings are just one tool in the entrepreneur's arsenal. They should be used strategically and in conjunction with other productivity strategies, such as time blocking, task batching, and prioritization. By mastering the art of meeting mastery and integrating it into your overall productivity toolkit, you can transform meetings from time-wasters into powerful catalysts for growth and success.

In conclusion, meetings don't have to be the bane of your entrepreneurial existence. With careful planning, effective facilitation, and a focus on outcomes, meetings can be transformed into valuable opportunities for collaboration, decision-making, and progress. By embracing the principles of meeting mastery, you can reclaim your time, boost your productivity, and achieve your entrepreneurial goals.

þþþ

Breaks are not a luxury; they're a necessity. Give your mind and body time to rest and recharge. A well-rested entrepreneur is a productive entrepreneur.

FIFTEEN

THE POWER OF BREAKS: RECHARGE FOR SUSTAINED PRODUCTIVITY.

In the relentless pursuit of entrepreneurial success, the notion of taking breaks might seem counterintuitive. The entrepreneurial spirit is often associated with unwavering dedication, long hours, and a relentless drive to achieve. However, the notion that productivity is directly proportional to the number of hours worked is a misconception. In reality, taking breaks is not a sign of weakness or laziness; it's a strategic investment in your long-term productivity and well-being.

Breaks, both short and long, play a crucial role in maintaining focus, boosting creativity, and preventing burnout. They provide an opportunity for your mind and body to rest and recharge, allowing you to return to your work with renewed energy and enthusiasm. In essence, breaks are not a distraction from work; they are an integral part of the work process.

The human brain is not designed for sustained focus. Research has shown that our attention span naturally wanes after a certain period of continuous work. This phenomenon, known as cognitive fatigue, can lead to decreased productivity, increased errors, and difficulty making decisions. Taking short breaks throughout the day can help to mitigate this fatigue and maintain optimal cognitive function.

Short breaks, typically lasting 5-15 minutes, can be surprisingly effective in restoring mental clarity and focus. They allow your brain to disengage from the task at hand and enter a state of rest. During this time, your subconscious mind can continue to process information and generate creative insights. When you return to your work, you'll often find that you're able to approach it with a fresh perspective and renewed energy.

The type of break you take can also impact its effectiveness. Engaging in activities that are completely unrelated to your work, such as taking a walk, listening to music, or having a casual conversation, can be particularly beneficial. These activities allow your mind to wander and make new connections, which can lead to creative breakthroughs.

Longer breaks, such as lunch breaks or even extended vacations, are equally important for sustained productivity. They provide an opportunity to disconnect from work completely and recharge your physical and mental batteries. During these breaks, it's important to prioritize activities that promote relaxation and well-being, such as spending time with loved ones, pursuing hobbies, or simply enjoying nature.

The benefits of taking breaks extend beyond improved focus and creativity. Research has shown that breaks can also reduce stress, improve mood, and boost overall well-being. When you're feeling stressed or overwhelmed, taking a short break can help to clear your head and reduce anxiety. Engaging in enjoyable activities during your breaks can also improve your mood and motivation, making it easier to tackle challenges and setbacks.

Incorporating breaks into your daily routine requires a conscious effort and a willingness to challenge conventional notions of productivity. It's easy to fall into the trap of working for hours on end without taking a break, especially when faced with tight deadlines or demanding workloads. However, this approach is ultimately counterproductive, as it can lead to burnout and decreased performance.

To make breaks a regular part of your work routine, it's helpful to schedule them in advance. This could involve setting a timer to remind you to take short breaks throughout the day or blocking out specific times for longer breaks. You can also use apps or software to help you track your breaks and ensure that you're taking them regularly.

The frequency and duration of your breaks will depend on your individual needs and preferences. Some people find that taking short breaks every hour or two is most effective, while others prefer to work for longer stretches with longer breaks in between. Experiment with different schedules and find what works best for you.

The key is to make breaks a non-negotiable part of your day. Treat them as important appointments that you wouldn't miss. By prioritizing your rest and recovery, you'll be investing in your long-term productivity and well-being. You'll be able to work smarter, not harder, and achieve greater success in your entrepreneurial endeavors.

ᗡᗡᗡ

Your morning and evening routines set the tone for your day. Design rituals that energize you, inspire you, and prepare you for the challenges ahead.

SIXTEEN

MORNING & EVENING ROUTINES: SET THE TONE FOR A PRODUCTIVE DAY.

The bookends of our days, the morning and evening routines, hold a unique power in shaping our lives. While often overlooked amidst the hustle and bustle of daily life, these routines can be transformative, setting the tone for productivity, focus, and overall well-being. For entrepreneurs, whose lives are often a whirlwind of challenges and opportunities, establishing effective morning and evening routines can be the key to unlocking their full potential.

Mornings, that sacred time before the demands of the day begin to clamor for attention, are a blank canvas upon which we can paint the masterpiece of our day. How we choose to spend those precious hours can have a profound impact on our mood, energy levels, and productivity throughout the day.

A well-structured morning routine can prime us for success by setting a positive and productive tone. It allows us to start the day with intention and purpose, rather than feeling rushed and overwhelmed. By incorporating activities that nourish our mind, body, and spirit, we can create a sense of calm and focus that will carry us through the day's challenges.

One of the most beneficial aspects of a morning routine is its ability to reduce decision fatigue. By establishing a set sequence of activities, we eliminate the need to make countless small decisions in the morning, freeing up mental energy for more important tasks. This can be particularly beneficial for entrepreneurs, who often face a barrage of decisions throughout the day.

Another advantage of a morning routine is its potential to boost productivity. By starting the day with focused and intentional activities, we create momentum that can carry us through the rest of the day. Whether it's tackling a challenging task, responding to emails, or attending meetings, we're more likely to approach these activities with energy and enthusiasm when we've started the day on the right foot.

The specific activities that make up a morning routine will vary from person to person. However, some common elements include exercise, meditation, journaling, reading, and eating a healthy breakfast. These activities can help to reduce stress, improve focus, boost creativity, and set a positive tone for the day.

Experimentation is key to finding a morning routine that works for you. Try different activities and see what feels most beneficial. The most important thing is to find a routine that you enjoy and that you can stick with consistently.

Just as a morning routine sets the stage for a productive day, an evening routine prepares us for a restful night and sets the stage for a productive tomorrow. It's a time to unwind, reflect on the day's accomplishments, and prepare for the challenges and opportunities that lie ahead.

One of the key benefits of an evening routine is its ability to promote relaxation and better sleep. By winding down with calming activities, such as reading, taking a warm bath, or listening to soothing music, we can signal to our bodies that it's time to rest. This can help us fall asleep more easily and enjoy a deeper, more restorative sleep.

An evening routine can also be a time for reflection and gratitude. By taking a few minutes to review the day's events and express gratitude for the good things that happened, we can cultivate a positive mindset and reduce stress. This can be particularly beneficial for entrepreneurs, who often face challenges and setbacks.

Preparing for the next day is another important aspect of an evening routine. By reviewing your calendar, preparing your to-do list, and laying out your clothes for the next day, you can minimize morning stress and ensure that you start the day feeling organized and in control.

Just as with your morning routine, experimentation is key to finding an evening routine that works for you. Try different activities and see what helps you relax and unwind. The most important thing is to find a routine that you enjoy and that you can stick with consistently.

It's also important to be flexible with your routines. There will be days when you have to deviate from your schedule due to unexpected events or commitments. Don't beat yourself up if you miss a day or two. Simply pick up where you left off and continue to prioritize your routines as much as possible.

By establishing effective morning and evening routines, you can create a framework for a more productive, fulfilling, and balanced life. These routines can help you reduce stress, improve focus, boost creativity, and achieve your goals. So, take the time to invest in your routines, and watch as your life transforms for the better.

ᚦᚦᚦ

Stress is the entrepreneur's silent saboteur. Prioritize self-care, manage your time effectively, and build a strong support network. A healthy entrepreneur is a successful entrepreneur.

SEVENTEEN

Stress Management: Avoid Burnout and Maintain High Performance.

The entrepreneurial journey is exhilarating yet demanding. The pursuit of innovation, growth, and success often comes with a hefty dose of stress. From long hours and tight deadlines to financial pressures and unexpected setbacks, the challenges of entrepreneurship can take a toll on even the most resilient individuals. Unmanaged stress can lead to burnout, a state of emotional, physical, and mental exhaustion that can significantly impact productivity, creativity, and overall well-being. Therefore, effective stress management is not just a luxury for entrepreneurs; it's a necessity.

Stress, in itself, is not inherently bad. In fact, a moderate amount of stress can be beneficial, motivating us to perform at our best. However, when stress becomes chronic and overwhelming, it can have detrimental effects on our health, relationships, and work performance. As an entrepreneur, it's crucial to develop healthy coping mechanisms and proactively manage stress to avoid burnout and maintain high performance.

The first step in managing stress is to identify your stressors. What are the specific situations, events, or thoughts that trigger stress for you? Is it the pressure to meet deadlines, the fear of failure, or the constant demands on your time? Once you understand your stressors, you can start to develop strategies for dealing with them.

One effective approach to stress management is to focus on self-care. This involves taking care of your physical, emotional, and mental health. Prioritize getting enough sleep, eating a healthy diet, and exercising regularly. These basic lifestyle habits can have a profound impact on your resilience to stress.

In addition to physical self-care, emotional self-care is equally important. Find healthy ways to express your emotions, whether it's talking to a friend or therapist, journaling, or engaging in creative activities. Meditation and mindfulness practices can also be effective in reducing stress and promoting emotional well-being.

Time management plays a crucial role in stress management. As an entrepreneur, you're likely juggling multiple responsibilities and deadlines. Learning to prioritize tasks, delegate effectively, and set realistic expectations can help to reduce the feeling of overwhelm and create a more manageable workload. Techniques like time blocking and the Pomodoro Technique can also be helpful in managing your time and reducing stress.

Building a strong support network is another essential aspect of stress management. Surround yourself with positive and supportive people who can offer encouragement, guidance, and perspective. This could include friends, family, mentors, or fellow entrepreneurs. Don't be afraid to ask for help when you need it.

Learning to say "no" is also crucial for managing stress. As an entrepreneur, you're likely to receive numerous requests and opportunities. While it's tempting to say "yes" to everything, it's important to be selective and prioritize commitments that align with your goals and values. Saying "no" to non-essential commitments can free up your time and energy for the things that truly matter.

Stress management is not a one-size-fits-all solution. What works for one person may not work for another. It's important to experiment with different strategies and find what works best for you. This might involve trying different relaxation techniques, seeking professional help, or simply taking some time for yourself each day to recharge.

Remember, stress management is an ongoing process. It's not something you do once and then forget about. It requires constant vigilance and a willingness to adapt as your circumstances change. By making stress management a priority, you can build resilience, prevent burnout, and maintain high performance in your entrepreneurial endeavors.

Stress is an inevitable part of the entrepreneurial journey. However, with effective stress management strategies, you can mitigate its negative impact and even harness it to your advantage. By prioritizing self-care, managing your time effectively, building a strong support network, and learning to say "no," you can create a more balanced and fulfilling entrepreneurial life. Remember, your well-being is not just a personal matter; it's a business imperative. When you're healthy, happy, and stress-free, you're more likely to be creative, productive, and successful. So, invest in your well-being and watch your entrepreneurial dreams flourish.

❦❦❦

Technology is your ally. Explore the vast array of time management apps and software available. Let them streamline your workflow and boost your efficiency.

EIGHTEEN

TOOLS OF THE TRADE: APPS AND SOFTWARE FOR TIME MANAGEMENT SUCCESS.

In the digital age, entrepreneurs have a wealth of tools at their disposal to streamline their workflows, enhance productivity, and achieve their goals. Among these tools, time management apps and software have emerged as indispensable assets for busy entrepreneurs seeking to optimize their time and achieve peak efficiency. These digital solutions offer a wide range of features and functionalities that can transform the way you manage your time, tasks, and projects.

One of the most fundamental time management tools is the calendar app. Whether it's Google Calendar, Outlook Calendar, or a specialized calendar app like Fantastical, these tools provide a centralized platform for scheduling appointments, meetings, deadlines, and other important events. With features like reminders, notifications, and shared calendars, you can stay on top of your schedule and collaborate with others seamlessly.

For managing tasks and to-do lists, task management apps like Todoist, Asana, and Trello are invaluable. These tools allow you to create and prioritize tasks, set deadlines, assign responsibilities, and track progress. With features like recurring tasks, subtasks, and integrations with other apps, you can create a comprehensive system for managing your workload and ensuring that nothing falls through the cracks.

Time tracking apps like Toggl, Harvest, and RescueTime provide detailed insights into how you're spending your time. These tools automatically track the time you spend on different tasks and activities, giving you a clear picture of your productivity patterns. By analyzing this data, you can identify time sinks, optimize your workflow, and make more informed decisions about how to allocate your time.

Project management tools like Basecamp, Monday.com, and ClickUp are essential for entrepreneurs who manage complex projects with multiple stakeholders. These tools provide a centralized platform for planning, organizing, and tracking projects. With features like task management, file sharing, communication channels, and progress tracking, you can keep all aspects of your projects in one place and ensure that everyone is on the same page.

Note-taking apps like Evernote, OneNote, and Notion are valuable tools for capturing ideas, organizing information, and collaborating with others. These apps allow you to create notes, checklists, documents, and even wikis. With features like cloud syncing, search functionality, and integrations with other apps, you can access your notes from anywhere and easily find the information you need.

Communication and collaboration tools like Slack, Microsoft Teams, and Zoom are essential for entrepreneurs who work with remote teams or collaborate with clients and partners. These tools provide real-time communication channels, video conferencing capabilities, and file-sharing options, enabling seamless collaboration regardless of location.

In addition to these general-purpose tools, there are also specialized apps and software designed for specific needs. For example, if you're struggling with procrastination, you can use apps like Focus@Will or Freedom to block distracting websites and apps. If you need help with time management and focus, you can try apps like Forest or Habitica, which gamify the process and provide rewards for completing tasks.

The sheer number of time management apps and software available can be overwhelming. To choose the right tools for your needs, it's important to consider your specific goals, workflow, and budget. Start by identifying the areas where you need the most help. Are you struggling with task management, time tracking, project management, or something else? Once you know what you need, you can start to research different tools and compare their features and pricing.

Don't be afraid to experiment with different tools to find what works best for you. Most apps offer free trials or freemium versions, so you can try them out before committing to a paid subscription. It's also important to remember that no single tool will solve all of your time management problems. The key is to find a combination of tools that work together to support your workflow and help you achieve your goals.

Integrating time management tools into your daily routine takes time and effort, but the benefits are well worth it. By automating repetitive tasks, tracking your time, managing projects, and collaborating with others more effectively, you can free up valuable time and energy to focus on what truly matters: growing your business and achieving your entrepreneurial dreams.

❦❦❦

The path to success is paved with continuous improvement. Embrace change, seek out new ideas, and never stop learning. Adaptation is key to entrepreneurial survival.

NINETEEN

CONTINUOUS IMPROVEMENT: ADAPT AND REFINE YOUR STRATEGIES.

In the dynamic landscape of entrepreneurship, where change is the only constant, the ability to adapt and evolve is paramount. Stagnation is not an option for those who seek to thrive in this ever-shifting terrain. Continuous improvement, a mindset and a methodology, is the key to unlocking long-term success. It's about constantly evaluating your strategies, identifying areas for growth, and making incremental changes that lead to significant results over time.

At its core, continuous improvement is a commitment to never settling for "good enough." It's a recognition that there's always room for growth, innovation, and optimization. This mindset is deeply ingrained in the entrepreneurial spirit, where the pursuit of excellence is a driving force. However, continuous improvement is not just about making changes for the sake of change; it's about making informed and intentional changes that are aligned with your goals and values.

The process of continuous improvement involves a cyclical approach of planning, doing, checking, and acting. This framework, often referred to as the PDCA cycle, provides a structured approach for identifying opportunities for improvement, implementing changes, evaluating their impact, and making further adjustments as needed.

The planning phase involves setting clear goals and objectives for improvement. What do you want to achieve? What are your key performance indicators (KPIs)? What are the specific areas where you want to see improvement? By defining your goals and objectives, you create a roadmap for your continuous improvement efforts.

The doing phase involves implementing the changes you've identified. This could involve introducing new processes, adopting new technologies, or training your team on new skills. The key is to start small and experiment with different approaches to see what works best for your business.

The checking phase involves evaluating the impact of your changes. Are they having the desired effect? Are they improving your KPIs? Are they meeting your goals and objectives? By collecting data and analyzing the results, you can gain valuable insights into the effectiveness of your efforts.

The acting phase involves making further adjustments based on the results of your evaluation. If the changes are working, you can scale them up or implement them in other areas of your business. If they're not working, you can identify the reasons for failure and make necessary modifications.

Continuous improvement is not a one-time event; it's an ongoing process. It requires a commitment to constantly learning, adapting, and evolving. This means staying abreast of industry trends, seeking out new ideas, and being open to feedback. It also means fostering a culture of continuous improvement within your organization, where everyone is encouraged to contribute ideas and suggestions.

One of the most powerful tools for continuous improvement is feedback. By actively seeking feedback from your customers, employees, and partners, you can gain valuable insights into your strengths and weaknesses. This feedback can help you identify areas for improvement, validate your assumptions, and make more informed decisions.

Another key tool for continuous improvement is data. By tracking your KPIs and analyzing your performance data, you can identify trends, measure progress, and make data-driven decisions. This data can also help you identify bottlenecks, inefficiencies, and opportunities for optimization.

Technology can also play a crucial role in continuous improvement. Numerous software tools and platforms are available to help you track your KPIs, analyze your data, and automate your processes. These tools can streamline your workflow, reduce errors, and free up your time for more strategic activities.

The benefits of continuous improvement are numerous. It can help you:

Increase efficiency: By identifying and eliminating bottlenecks, you can streamline your processes and improve efficiency.

Reduce costs: By optimizing your operations, you can reduce waste and lower your costs.

Improve quality: By continuously monitoring your processes and making adjustments, you can improve the quality of your products and services.

Enhance customer satisfaction: By listening to your customers and addressing their needs, you can enhance customer satisfaction and loyalty.

Boost employee morale: By empowering your employees to contribute to the improvement process, you can boost morale and engagement.

Stay ahead of the competition: By continuously innovating and adapting, you can stay ahead of the competition and maintain a competitive edge.

Continuous improvement is not just a methodology; it's a way of life for entrepreneurs who seek to thrive in a constantly changing world. It's about embracing change, seeking out new ideas, and constantly striving to improve. By making continuous improvement a core part of your entrepreneurial DNA, you can build a resilient and adaptable business that's poised for long-term success.

ppp

Teamwork makes the dream work. Foster a culture of time management within your organization. Encourage collaboration, communication, and accountability.

TWENTY

TIME MANAGEMENT FOR TEAMS: BOOST PRODUCTIVITY ACROSS YOUR ORGANIZATION.

In the intricate machinery of a successful organization, time management is not merely an individual pursuit, but a collective endeavor. The productivity of a team, and subsequently the entire organization, is intrinsically linked to how effectively its members manage their time. While individual time management skills are undoubtedly important, fostering a culture of time management across the organization is paramount for achieving sustained high performance and optimal results.

At its core, team time management involves aligning individual efforts with shared goals and deadlines. It's about creating a synchronized workflow where each member understands their role, responsibilities, and the impact their actions have on the overall progress. Effective team time management requires a combination of clear communication, collaboration, accountability, and the right tools and processes.

One of the fundamental pillars of team time management is setting clear and measurable goals. These goals should be aligned with the overall vision and mission of the organization, and they should be communicated effectively to all team members. By establishing clear goals, teams create a sense of purpose and direction, ensuring that everyone is working towards a common objective.

Once the goals are set, it's crucial to break them down into smaller, more manageable tasks and assign them to specific team members. This task allocation should be based on individual strengths and skills, ensuring that each person is working on tasks that they are best suited for. This not only optimizes productivity but also fosters a sense of ownership and accountability.

Effective communication is the lifeblood of team time management. Regular team meetings, check-ins, and progress reports are essential for keeping everyone informed and aligned. These communication channels provide a platform for sharing updates, discussing challenges, and brainstorming solutions. They also foster a sense of camaraderie and collaboration, which can significantly boost morale and productivity.

Transparency is another crucial aspect of team time management. When team members have visibility into each other's work, it fosters a sense of trust and accountability. Project management tools like Asana, Trello, or Basecamp can be invaluable for creating transparency by providing a centralized platform for tracking progress, sharing updates, and collaborating on tasks.

Deadlines are the heartbeat of any project. They create a sense of urgency and ensure that tasks are completed on time. However, setting realistic deadlines is equally important. Unrealistic deadlines can lead to stress, burnout, and ultimately, decreased productivity. It's important to involve team members in the deadline-setting process to ensure that they are feasible and achievable.

In addition to deadlines, regular reviews and feedback sessions are crucial for keeping projects on track and ensuring that everyone is aligned. These sessions provide an opportunity to assess progress, identify bottlenecks, and make necessary adjustments. They also allow team members to provide feedback, share insights, and learn from each other's experiences.

Empowering team members is another key element of effective time management. When individuals feel empowered to make decisions, take ownership of their tasks, and contribute their ideas, they are more likely to be engaged and motivated. This can lead to increased productivity, innovation, and overall team performance.

To foster empowerment, it's important to create a culture of trust and respect. This involves providing team members with the autonomy to make decisions, the resources they need to succeed, and the support to overcome challenges. It also involves recognizing and rewarding their contributions and creating a safe space for them to share their ideas and concerns.

Technology can be a powerful ally in team time management. Numerous tools and software are available to help teams streamline their workflows, automate tasks, and collaborate more effectively. Project management tools, communication platforms, time tracking software, and calendar apps can all play a vital role in enhancing team productivity.

However, technology is not a silver bullet. The most sophisticated tools will be ineffective if the underlying processes are flawed or if the team lacks the skills and discipline to use them effectively. Therefore, it's crucial to invest in training and development to ensure that your team has the necessary skills to leverage technology to its full potential.

The benefits of effective team time management are far-reaching. It can lead to increased productivity, improved efficiency, reduced costs, enhanced collaboration, and ultimately, a more successful and profitable organization. By prioritizing time management and making it a core part of your organizational culture, you can create a high-performing team that's capable of achieving remarkable results.

Time management is not just an individual skill; it's a team sport. By fostering a culture of time management, setting clear goals, communicating effectively, embracing transparency, setting realistic deadlines, empowering team members, and leveraging technology, you can unlock the full potential of your team and drive your organization towards greater success.

ᐅᐅᐅ

Work-life balance is not a myth. It's a conscious choice. Set boundaries, prioritize your well-being, and make time for the things that matter most.

TWENTY-ONE

PRODUCTIVITY UNLEASHED: YOUR ROADMAP TO ENTREPRENEURIAL SUCCESS.

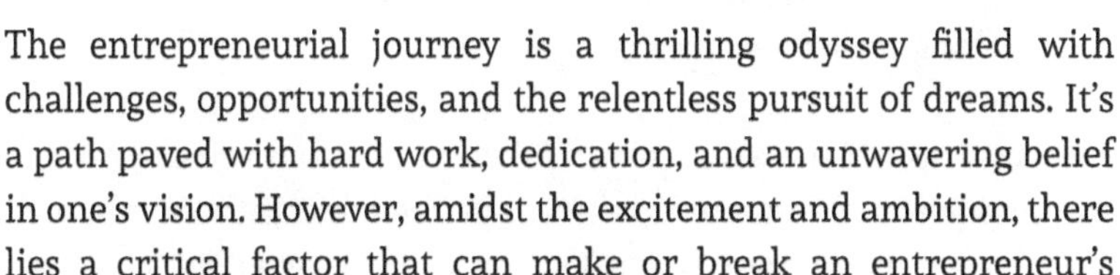

The entrepreneurial journey is a thrilling odyssey filled with challenges, opportunities, and the relentless pursuit of dreams. It's a path paved with hard work, dedication, and an unwavering belief in one's vision. However, amidst the excitement and ambition, there lies a critical factor that can make or break an entrepreneur's success: productivity.

Productivity, in the entrepreneurial context, is not merely about working harder or longer hours. It's about working smarter, maximizing efficiency, and achieving optimal results with the resources at hand. It's about identifying and focusing on high-impact activities, eliminating time-wasters, and creating a sustainable workflow that fosters both personal and professional growth.

The entrepreneurial landscape is a breeding ground for distractions and competing priorities. From the constant influx of emails and meetings to the pressure of managing finances and building a team, entrepreneurs face a myriad of demands on their time and attention. Without a clear roadmap for productivity, it's easy to become overwhelmed, lose focus, and ultimately, derail your progress.

This roadmap begins with a fundamental shift in mindset. Productivity is not a destination; it's a journey. It's an ongoing process of learning, adapting, and refining your approach. It's about embracing new tools and techniques, experimenting with different strategies, and continuously seeking ways to improve.

Goal setting is the compass that guides this journey. By defining clear, measurable, and achievable goals, you create a sense of purpose and direction. Your goals should be aligned with your overall vision and mission, and they should be broken down into smaller, more manageable steps. This provides a roadmap for your daily activities, ensuring that every task you undertake contributes to your long-term objectives.

Prioritization is the art of distinguishing between the urgent and the important. As an entrepreneur, you're constantly bombarded with demands on your time. It's crucial to develop the ability to discern which tasks are truly essential for achieving your goals and which ones can be delegated, delayed, or eliminated altogether. This requires a deep understanding of your business, your priorities, and your strengths.

Time management is the engine that powers your productivity. It's about allocating your time effectively, minimizing distractions, and optimizing your workflow. Techniques like time blocking, task batching, and the Pomodoro Technique can help you structure your day, maintain focus, and avoid burnout. It's also important to be mindful of your energy levels and work when you're most productive.

Delegation and outsourcing are powerful tools for freeing up your time and leveraging the expertise of others. By entrusting certain tasks to capable team members or external partners, you can focus on your core competencies and strategic initiatives. This not only enhances your productivity but also empowers your team and fosters a culture of collaboration.

Automation is another key element of productivity unleashed. By harnessing the power of technology, you can streamline repetitive tasks, reduce errors, and free up valuable time for more creative and strategic work. From email automation and social media scheduling to data analysis and customer relationship management, there are countless tools available to help you automate your workflow and boost your efficiency.

Continuous improvement is the cornerstone of sustainable productivity. It's about constantly evaluating your strategies, identifying areas for growth, and making incremental changes that lead to significant results over time. By embracing a mindset of learning and adaptability, you can stay ahead of the curve and maintain a competitive edge.

The roadmap to entrepreneurial success is not a straight line. It's a winding path filled with twists, turns, and unexpected detours. However, by mastering the principles of productivity, you can navigate this path with confidence and grace. By setting clear goals, prioritizing effectively, managing your time wisely, delegating strategically, embracing automation, and committing to continuous improvement, you can unlock your full potential, achieve your dreams, and make a lasting impact on the world.

Productivity is not just a means to an end; it's a way of life. It's about creating a sustainable and fulfilling lifestyle that allows you to achieve your goals while maintaining your well-being. It's about finding the balance between work and play, between ambition and contentment. By embracing productivity as a lifestyle, you can not only achieve entrepreneurial success but also create a life that you love.

Productivity is not a destination; it's a journey. Embrace the challenges, celebrate the victories, and never stop striving for excellence.

TWENTY-TWO
SUMMARY

In the dynamic and demanding world of entrepreneurship, time is the most precious asset one possesses. Mastering its management is crucial for achieving success, fostering well-being, and ultimately, unlocking one's full potential. This summary encapsulates the key strategies and principles discussed throughout this book, providing a comprehensive roadmap for entrepreneurs to navigate the complexities of time management and unleash their productivity.

At the heart of entrepreneurial time management lies the understanding that time is a finite resource, and every minute invested (or wasted) has a direct impact on the trajectory of one's business and life. The "entrepreneurial clock" ticks differently than a traditional 9-to-5 job, demanding constant attention and the ability to discern between urgent and important tasks.

Goal setting acts as the compass guiding this journey. It's not merely about creating a wishlist, but a strategic process involving SMART goals: Specific, Measurable, Achievable, Relevant, and Time-bound. These goals serve as beacons, illuminating the path towards desired outcomes and providing motivation, direction, and benchmarks for measuring progress.

Prioritization, the art of doing less but achieving more, is another cornerstone of effective time management. The 80/20 rule, or Pareto Principle, reminds us that a small fraction of our efforts often yields the majority of results. By identifying these high-impact activities and focusing our energy on them, we can significantly enhance our productivity and effectiveness.

Time blocking, a powerful technique for structuring our day, involves dividing it into specific blocks dedicated to particular tasks or activities. This approach minimizes distractions, improves focus, and ensures that our most important priorities receive adequate attention. Task batching, on the other hand, streamlines workflow by grouping similar tasks together, reducing context switching and enhancing efficiency.

Energy management is about working smarter, not harder. By understanding our natural energy rhythms and aligning our tasks accordingly, we can maximize our output during peak periods and rest or engage in less demanding tasks during lulls. This approach prevents burnout, improves focus, and ensures sustainable productivity.

The Pomodoro Technique offers a structured approach to combat procrastination and enhance focus. By breaking down work into intervals, traditionally 25 minutes in length, separated by short breaks, it helps maintain energy levels, prevent burnout, and improve overall productivity.

Delegation and outsourcing are strategic tools for leveraging the power of others. By entrusting tasks to capable team members or external partners, entrepreneurs can focus on their core competencies and strategic initiatives, accelerating growth and achieving a healthier work-life balance.

Automation, the harnessing of technology to streamline repetitive tasks, is a game-changer for entrepreneurs. By automating mundane and time-consuming activities, businesses can improve efficiency, reduce errors, and free up valuable time for more strategic endeavors.

Saying "no" is an art that protects our time from non-essential commitments. In a world overflowing with opportunities, it's crucial to be discerning and prioritize activities that align with our goals and values. By learning to say "no" gracefully and tactfully, we can safeguard our time and focus on what truly matters.

Creating a focus-friendly environment is essential for minimizing distractions and maximizing productivity. This involves eliminating or minimizing distractions, decluttering our workspace, optimizing our physical environment, and managing our mental state. By cultivating a space that promotes focus and concentration, we can unlock our full potential and achieve our goals.

Time tracking and analysis provide valuable insights into how we're spending our time. By meticulously logging our activities and analyzing the data, we can identify time sinks, optimize our schedules, and make more informed decisions about our time allocation.

Meeting mastery is about transforming meetings from time-wasters into productive and efficient sessions. By setting clear goals, creating agendas, inviting the right people, utilizing technology effectively, and soliciting feedback, we can ensure that meetings contribute to our progress and success.

The power of breaks lies in their ability to recharge our minds and bodies, leading to sustained productivity and improved well-being. By incorporating short breaks throughout the day and longer breaks for rest and relaxation, we can prevent burnout, enhance focus, and boost creativity.

Morning and evening routines are the bookends of our days, setting the tone for productivity and well-being. By establishing consistent routines that nourish our mind, body, and spirit, we can start and end each day with intention, purpose, and a sense of control.

Stress management is essential for avoiding burnout and maintaining high performance. By identifying our stressors, practicing self-care, managing our time effectively, building a strong support network, and learning to say "no," we can mitigate the negative impact of stress and create a more balanced and fulfilling life.

This summary encapsulates the key principles and strategies for unleashing productivity in the entrepreneurial realm. By embracing these practices and adapting them to your unique needs and circumstances, you can optimize your time, achieve your goals, and create a thriving business and a fulfilling life. Remember, productivity is not a destination; it's an ongoing journey of continuous improvement and self-discovery.

Unleash your productivity, ignite your passion, and embrace the entrepreneurial adventure. Your future is yours to create.

Citation And References

This book represents the culmination of extensive research and meticulous analysis, incorporating a diverse range of sources, including numerous books, scholarly studies, and personal experiences. Additionally, I have scoured various websites to gather relevant information and data essential for the compilation of this work. I have taken every precaution to ensure the accuracy of the information presented and have diligently cited all sources to acknowledge their contributions.

Despite these efforts, the possibility of inadvertent errors remains. I deeply value the insights of my readers and appreciate any feedback that can help identify and rectify such inaccuracies. I encourage you to bring any discrepancies to my attention.

Your feedback is not only welcome but crucial, as it will aid in correcting current editions and enhancing the content of future ones. I am committed to maintaining the highest standards of accuracy and reliability in my work and thank you for your support and understanding.

Additionally, I firmly uphold the principle of freedom of speech and expression as guaranteed under Article 19(1)(a) of the Constitution of India, and I respect the diverse viewpoints and expressions of all readers.

ᗡᗡᗡ

Other Books Of The Author

1. Empowering Minds: A Journey into Women's Self-Discovery and Power
2. The Dynamics of Motivation: Catalyzing Thought into Action
3. Meditation and Mental Well Being: The Path to Inner Peace and Clarity
4. The Psychology of Child Education: Nurturing Future Generations
5. Ethical Enlightenment: A Modern Guide to Living with Integrity
6. Voices of Empowerment: Stories of Women Rising Against Odds
7. Social Psychology in Everyday Life: Understanding Human Connections
8. The Essence of Motivational Speaking: Inspiring Change in Others
9. Balancing Acts: Women, Work, and the Will to Lead
10. Guiding with Grace: Raising Children with Compassion and Awareness
11. The Power of Positive Aging: Embracing Life After Fifty
12. Building Resilient Communities: Social Work in Action
13. The Ethical Educator: Principles for Teaching and Learning
14. From Insight to Impact: Social Psychology for a Better World
15. The Ethics of Empathy: A Guide to Ethical Living
16. The Science of Empowering the Self: Navigating Life's Challenges with Psychological Wisdom
17. The Mindful Conscious Leader: Meditation Techniques for Modern Management
18. Pioneering Spirit: Women's Pathways to Leadership and Empowerment
19. Feeling to Healing: The Role of Emotional Intelligence in Child Development
20. Transformative Talks and Words of Inspiration: Insights into Motivational Oratory

in a Complex World

46. Secret of Solopreneur's Odyssey: Navigating the Path to Self-Employment
47. Exploring Tapestry of Peace: Global Perspectives on Harmony
48. The Art and Actions of Connection: Mastering Communication for Impact
49. She Governs and at the Helm: Strategies for Political Empowerment
50. Rising Above and Rising with Grace: A Woman's Roadmap to Career Mastery
51. The Effect of Networking & Connectedness: Building Strategic Alliances for Women
52. Beyond his Barriers: Women Thriving in Male-Dominated Fields
53. Secret of Inner Compass: Navigating Life with Intuition
54. Creative & Pro-Active Muses: A Celebration of Women in the Arts
55. Unburdened: The Art of Releasing the Past
56. Amplified Voices: Speeches of Women that Astonished the World
57. Secret of Manifesting Dreams: A Woman's Guide to Intentional Living
58. Ethics and Value Based Education: Reimagining Japan's School System
59. The Moral Compass Curriculum: A Holistic Approach
60. Tech with Heart: Integrating Ethics into Digital Learning
61. Honoring Virtue: Recognizing Ethical Excellence in Education
62. Raising Good Humans: A Guide to Character Development
63. The Spark Within: Nurturing Creativity in Children
64. The Teenager Whisperer: Navigating Adolescence with Grace
65. Igniting a Passion for Learning: Inspiring Lifelong Curiosity
66. The Habit Lab: Cultivating Positive Behaviors in Children
67. Seeds of Empathy: Fostering Compassion in Young Hearts
68. The Reading Revolution: Inspiring a Love of Books in Children
69. The Learning Brain: Unlocking the Secrets of Student Success
70. Teaching for All: Differentiated Instruction Strategies
71. The Time Alchemist: Mastering Time Management for Peak Performance

Bhajan
101. Pilgrimage of the Soul: Spiritual Journeys in India

❦❦❦

Contact

Dr. Minakshi Bansal
Social Activist
Ahmedabad, Gujarat, Bharat
minakshiindiag20@yahoo.com

❧❧❧

|| LOKAHA SAMASTHAHA SUKHINO BHAVANTU ||